From Smog to Fog - Traversing The Roads of Clouds and Mist.

Imran Khan

BookLeaf Publishing

Presentation by *BookLeaf Publishing*

Web: www.bookleafpub.com

E-mail: info@bookleafpub.com

ISBN: 9789357442541

First edition 2023

Robot

Have you ever seen a child who cries? Tears of
distress that receive cold replies?

Given the cold shoulder as the adult denies.
Pointing their finger saying: "Shut up! You are
full of lies!".

The pain and the hurt, of being treated like dirt.

"Come along now you little squirt!", dragging
me hard by the collar of my shirt.

"Lies!", they shout.
"Lies!", they chant.
"Nothing but lies!".

I wipe away quickly at my watery eyes, whilst
inside I'm angry and their behaviour I despise.

"Is everything always to do with logic and
having to rationalise?"
"Why are my feelings and emotions repeatedly
shooed away like flies?"

Inside I go numb, feeling quite dumb.

What a horrible place of doom and demise!
Ridiculed for every mistake no matter how hard one tries!

Am I supposed to put on some kind of a disguise?
Stop being human and start to mechanise,
become a robot and forever digitise??

This feels so wrong, and won't last long.

Pitter Patter Inner Chatter

Pitter patter, what's the matter?
Pitter patter, I feel flatter.

What's the matter? It's my inner chatter.
What's the matter? My thoughts going ratter tatter.

It's my inner chatter, feeding my worries from thinner to fatter.
It's my inner chatter, repeatedly over and over again it will natter.

Is it the former or is it the latter, that cover me like a batter?
Is it the former or is it the latter, that scurry and scatter?

Pitter patter, oh I don’t know it doesn’t matter!
Pitter patter, oh dear what is it with all this clatter!

Here I am, caught between the former and the latter!

Pitter patter, I sound as mad as a hatter!
Pitter patter, here we go again with the inner chatter!

Pressure

The pressure builds and will compress, pushing
and pressing till duress.

What a state, abort or abate.
I'm irate, get it off my plate!

Crushing stress, make it less!
Intense distress, now digress.

Distraction is the reaction.
An action of redaction.

Reflection to refraction, inflection and
detraction.

Withdrawal and holding back, a condition of
lack.

Desperate in despair, pulling out my hair. Crying
out "it's not fair!".
Now I'm bald, my head is bare!

In pitch black, fearing an attack.
Zip up my anorak, find that old shack.

A space to release, get some peace.

Seedling

Consider faith as a seed.
Surrounded by many a weed.

Faith requires nurturing and attention, planting a
beautiful flower with care and intention.

It needs space, give it some room.
A cultivated place, so it can bloom.

With growth comes pain, and periods of rain.

Inside each of us is a garden.
The heart in our chest which will either soften or
harden.

If it is cleaned and regularly cleared, then of
hardness and coldness it will be spared.

Find time to nurture this light, to help you
through your plight.

Within you find deep strength of inner might,
helpful wisdom and rich insight.

An inner rudder, at which we tend to shudder.

We'd rather not look within, and carry on the sin.

Afraid of openin, what we've been coverin.

Suppressin and repressin.
Dismissin and neglectin.

Just like the 'g' that has gone missin.

Until we face, our inner space.
We cannot find composure, nor proper closure.
Neither calmness nor truthful grace, until we unleash from our inner place.

Take your time, it's not a race.
You're doing just fine, you'll find your pace.

Having courage to be a beginner, will not make you any less of a winner.

You're on a learning curve - At times we skid and at times we swerve.

Accelerate a bit and then slow down.
A balanced speed achieves the crown.

Soul

On the dole, like a hot coal.
Burning sensation, representing deprivation.

Inside I churn, how will I earn.
Lacking provision, still no decision.

Things stir, it's all a blur.

What is my goal? Where is my aim?
Do I know my role? Is this a game?

This is the question, requiring digestion.

Open up to influence and further suggestion,
new perspectives will clear congestion.

Self reflection. Deep introspection.
Mining through the many layers.
Easing hardship with thorough prayers.

What is my aim? What is my role?
Distinguished an objective? Determined a goal?

Yearning to be creative, reconnecting with what
is native.

My many colours and various shades, painted
via transactions and different trades.

Obstructions and blockades, a series of parades.

To find facts and shed facades, do consistent
inner work over decades.

Dig through dirt with shovels and spades,
stripping away the masquerades.

Depart from vanity, because that's insanity.

No more scattering, stop spreading thin.
Enough with the splattering, that's stuff for the
bin.

Open up the bud and let it bloom.
Away with doom as well as gloom.

Sweep the heart clean, widen its beam.
Sense out my stream, follow the dream.

Open up the inner treasure, a gradual pathway
for immense pleasure.

Rediscovering my soul, the journey of returning
whole.

This is my purpose, this is my role.
I've found my aim, I've voiced my goal.

Express my spirit, unleash my soul.

Life on the Inside

Life gave me no choice except to look inwardly
for peace and satisfaction, as I couldn't find it
outwardly in any amusement or distraction.

All I found when I looked outside, were fleeting
indulgences to stimulate a joyride.

Frustration and dissatisfaction took hold over
and over, even if I drunk hard to the point of
hangover.

Just never content, no matter how many laws I
bent, or money I spent.
The "pleasure" just went, leaving me discontent.

Whenever I hoped and expected, I was
disappointed and quickly dejected.
Inwardly I protested, outwardly I projected.

My wishing and longing that I presumed as
"hope", was nothing but a spiral down an
uneven slope.

Burning my hands as I slide down the loose rope - slipping and ripping the harder I'm gripping.

Every time I try, things go awry.

Nothing more than an illusion, the more I indulge the more pain and confusion.

Followed by a realisation and conclusion:

Since I cannot find what I am looking for anywhere externally, then what is being sought must have been buried deep down embedded internally.

Having sunk there over a number of long childhood years, hidden under layers of negative conditioning and self consuming fears.

Living a life based on assumptions and scar-induced scares, including prejudices towards catastrophising and dreaming up nightmares.

Little did I realise my contribution and the climbed stairs, due to being heavily engrossed in sighs and despairs.

Wet eyes streaming weird soggy dribbling tears.
An inner dialogue of "Nobody cares!".

As I wash my face and brush my hair, I awaken
to the need for inner repair.

To clarify my sight, finding advantageous
height. Seeing what's right, making room for
growth and insight.

Throughout the climb, yes there is a lot of grime.
But hey I'm finding new meaning through
rhythm and rhyme.
Listen to the words - hear the chyme! Thank
God, Just in time!

Heart

My heart is being called to glisten and to shine,
as it beats and circulates nutrients just fine.

Attention is an action of the heart, this is the
place to start.

The light of consciousness on a seed, pure
loving water fulfilling dire need.

Like any living creature, it's a significant
feature.

Avoidance is misdeed, distance starts to mislead.
Compensated by greed - including other types of
thorny weed.
Leading one to spiritually bleed.

The wound from a hissing razor, delivers the
shock of an electric taser.
Infections of bitterness and sicknesses of envy,
drives one destitute and into a frenzy.

This is the leak, why a person is weak.
An illness of sarcasm, and ongoing cheek.

Of their strong fumes such people reek, a rotting smell like gone off leek.

That's how the heart will decay and recede, a grievous tragedy of suppression indeed.

There is always something more, things I haven't taken the time to fully explore.

In a place often given little attention and not wanting to bear, it seems digging deeper within is something to which I skeptically glare.
Going inside I would not dare, assuming the time and effort is too much to spare.
"Argh, what a nightmare".

That is, until life gave me no choice and said "take your share".
"It's yours, dear".

As I gradually approach and continue drawing near, I still feel a sudden fear.
Courage is to do things despite the fear feeling, because that's the way to break through the fear ceiling.

Though viscerally I may be reeling, and at times I am on the floor kneeling, progress is in these layers that I am peeling.

As momentum is generated, and the past is exonerated.

Only once I start to look within, can my real journey honestly begin.

Perspective

They called in for a back up squad, whilst
looking up at the heavens praying to God.

We need full support, send a cohort!

Come on now I need a report?! Or we'll have to
use our last resort!

Do you copy?! Over??!

The Tides are getting choppy!!
We're in Dover!!!

Abandon ship! No time to slip!
Life boats ready! C'mon hold steady!

We are sinking! This ship is drinking!
Wait! Look ahead, something is blinking!

Re ... relief? G-g-gosh .. b-beggars b-belief!

That the help we radioed in?!
Radio Crackles "Received aye, are yous the
Captin?"

As the fleet of RNLI lifeguards arrived, at once
the crew knew they had survived.

Glad they had neither drowned nor died, at last a
huge relief they breathed and they sighed.

A big weight has been lifted, and to a new state
they are shifted.

Imagine how without the help they were gifted,
far out to sea they would have drifted, piles of
wreckage needing to be sifted.

Assistance is always going to be on the way,
even if there is some minor delay.

So since that day, in awe they lay.
In being saved, a path is paved.

Take action, yes - get out of the mess.
And trust too, what is meant for you.

Desert Heat

It digs its roots deep, no matter how steep.

Stability is not cheap, fruits straightaway you do not reap.

Day you work and night you sleep, that kind of labour is way too cheap.

What if the day you slept and the night you worked? During light you rest and in darkness you perked?

When the heat is too hot, and the cool breeze is your slot.

The night time shadow, is not for the shallow.
Think of a cactus and not a mallow.

Producing sweet water, even in the deserts driest and most empty quarter.

How? Wow!

That is the capacity of a plant.
So do not tell me that a human can't.

Out

Will I be taken seriously and heard out? Or will I
feel a desperate impulse to scream and to shout?

Is it possible to let it all blowout?
There's always the risk of getting a clout!

Tension builds, desiring dissociation from the
guilds.

Suffocated and submerged, a need to be purged!
For too long with toxicity have I been merged!

Swimming about, like a helpless trout.
In the deep end feeling stuck, running repeatedly
into a muck.

This horrible bout of spinning like a waterspout,
turns me grey like grit and rough like grout.

Hard and edgy, unkempt and hedgy.

I need to bailout, before I blackout. Have to
breakout, prior to burnout.

Holdout making sense of the layout, so I can
map a way out.

The Ocean Within

I could not find peace or contentment or satisfaction in anything externally, so I resolved to dig deep within and find it internally.

To get the shovel out, and start shifting earth about.
Unfulfilled and discontent in turmoil, I turned inward and dug through the soil.

To do so initially felt bitter, and my impulse was to check Instagram or Twitter.
Instant gratification, a troublesome provocation.

I kept composure, and got closure.
As I dug for life inside, I started to enjoy the ride.

The inner world has a softness, an indulgence that has a fondness.
An ocean within became apparent, and my inner lens grew clearer and transparent.

A deep ocean of profound depth and magnitude within, this isn't how I expected it would all begin!

The first sign of water: moisture no doubt!
Then “droplets of water!” I exclaimed with a shout!
Streams and rivers began to spout, gushing forth from a reservoir that had to let it all out!

An inner ocean that replenishes, and never diminishes.
One that only grows greater with attention, the more I engage and make of it regular mention.

An ocean that tastes sweet, more palatable than an edible treat!

One where I find reflection and insight, a place of integrity and delight.

I feel neither fear nor fright, furthermore no need for fight and flight.

Instead I now pause rather than freeze, as I stand on the shores exposed to the cool breeze.

Spending time outside at sea, gave me the courage to go inside and see.
Beyond the debris.

More is less?

If less is more, then is more ... less?
What's your guess?

Hmmm, well I would say more or less. Would
you like a game of chess?

How about first we clear up this mess?
Because in my opinion more brings stress!
I don't want more because I'd rather have less!

OK fine the same I will confess.
Interesting, finally some progress.

Say no more, you've opened the door.

Less means there is more to bless, and we lose
that blessing when we digress. The trouble is
that sometimes we want more only to impress, to
appear to others like we are a prince or a
princess.

When in reality we are not, and to claim that is a
lot.

So more, breaks the law. Leaving us numb and stalling us raw.

More: often brings distress, as the burden of lies pile up under duress.

Things we grew up believing, all this time we've been projecting not perceiving!

True wealth is in giving not receiving, in never defrauding or being deceiving!

I'm shocked and surprised, how much was disguised!
Appalled that I never knew, the extent of what's actually untrue!

Five

No willpower and no drive, how on earth will I arrive?

For five seconds I inhale, holding it for another five before exhale.

Counting the breaths to five, and finding that I am still alive.

I didn't have to strain, nor put myself through pain.

Rather than push myself to the max, I took some time to unwind and relax.

The days cannot always be sunny, there are times it needs to rain.
I really am not being funny, this truly is life's game.

In managing and training, is the art of navigating and taming.

Clarity guides to reframe.
Learning from what I should refrain, and where I uncover my true gain.

To travel on a true lane, traversing my original authentic terrain.

Composure I regain, clearer becomes my aim.

I am not in it for fame, only a sincere objective clear and plain.

There are many things you and I will survive,
because of a purpose for which we are still alive.

Learn where to strive, and in what not to contrive.
Where to go live, if you truly seek to thrive.

Friend

A friend, is someone upon whom I sometimes
rely and also depend.

Someone to be real with and not pretend.
One that has my back and will protect and
defend.

Time together we often spend, even when apart
the text messages we send, are for planning what
to do the following weekend.

When I am in need - their hand they lend.
When I feel broken - their support is a Godsend.

Thank you dear friend, for helping me on the
mend.

We may at times drive each other around the
bend, getting competitive in ways provoking us
to contend, involving jokes and jibes that may
offend, though later we find it in ourselves to
reconcile and amend.

A friendship is a relationship to which we need
to attend, to keep it alight until the very end.

Angry and Annoyed

I'm angry and annoyed, when people assume
life is all about being employed.

Working nine to five, at home late I arrive.
Just to survive, do it all again and back to work I drive.

Is this life? Barely see my kids or my family and not even my wife?

Get home late, she's irate.
"Where've you been?! It's eleven seventeen!"

"Sorry" I say.
"It's just another day".

"Why the delay?!"
"You've no time for play, hardly get a holiday."
"Is this how things will stay?"

"You're right" I say.
"We need to find another way".

She feels angry and annoyed, as she too knows my void.

She understands when I'm running on empty, and how things changed so much since we were twenty.

We thought we had time, we were doing just fine.

Until no more could we bare, by thirty we had grey hair.
We thought "it's not fair", and said to ourselves "dear oh dear".

We need space, we need air.
To find our place, to reunite as a pair.

We feel angry and annoyed, because we don't want to go down under or be destroyed.

Like this it cannot remain, dwindling from remorse down to disdain.

We are a twin flame, that keep each other sane.
The spirit of our relationship we want to sustain.

Free from guilt, free from blame. Smoother than silt, liberated from shame.

Acknowledge the blockage, address the pain.

What has interfered and hugely disrupted?
Obstacles have twisted and largely corrupted?

There's more behind these embers of anger,
under the ashes is a cliffhanger.

Decision Time

"Move! You've got nothing to prove!"

I woke up from my sleep, and started to weep.
That's such a big leap! That's just too deep!

As I cried, I feel like I've lied.
Something is being denied.

I turned on my side, restlessly wondering about
the bumpy ride.

What lies ahead, is what I dread.

The uncertainty and the unknown, is why I
procrastinate and postpone.

For hours I scroll through my phone, usually
when I'm alone.
I'll be at home, sitting in one place like a stone.

As idle as a grey rock, whilst I watch videos on
Tiktok.

My time is limited, and I feel inhibited.

Fed up and withdrawn, full of bitterness and scorn.

Grass is only green when people water their lawn.
Otherwise it dries, turning from green to fawn.

As my heart opens up a peep, the tears of my fears into my clothes now seep.

Absorbed up in a sponge, from head to heart I now plunge.

The truly smart, follow their heart.

I start to smile, working through my denial.

This is my test, this is my trial.
Give it the best, inspiration dial.

Writing

Phases of writing, are stages of igniting.

My heart in motion, dedicated with devotion.

The momentum of an ocean, a vast sea of emotion.

I begin to write, and flames start to ignite.

Feelings so profound, lifting me off the ground.
Tuning in to this inner sound, lingering and staying around.

A state that is elusive, yet deeply encompassing and highly inclusive.

The richness of flow, springs forth from deep below.

A fire in the belly, packs a big welly.

I'm no longer empty, no longer hollow. Now with plenty, far from shallow.

Your Story

Tell me your story, in all its glory.
Your job is expression, not apprehension.

To exhibit, not inhibit.
What goes inside, must return outside.

We inhale, to exhale.
We reflect, when we introspect.

Give yourself space for your soul's intercession,
so it inspires and guides your next writing
session.

With in-built strength you transcend repression,
as finding and discovering yourself alleviates
depression.

Be gentle and compassionate enough to give
some concession, as you work your way through
this new true profession.

In honesty and confession, there's development
and progression.

Every opportunity, is for inner utility.
To weave the soft thread, and the hard outer shell shed.

Caterpillars go into a cocoon, coming out as butterflies throughout the monsoon.

It is your story we all want to read. Starting to write it out will help you proceed, as this is how you dig out your inner seed.

You remove the weed, to allow your spirit to feed.
On the light of attention, which releases the tension.

The key is your intention - it is not engineered nor by invention.

Put your words down on paper, your soul will be the shaper.

We cannot read if you do not write, so do us a favour and share your insight - your inner spark your passion will ignite.
We all have a battle and all choose a fight, thus we all too need a bit of respite.
We are all humans with periods of plight, as well as many moments of various delight.

Exercise and loosen up so you are not so tight.
Stars twinkle beautifully in the darkest night.

Do not worry if you are “wrong” or if you are “right”.
Just share with us your intuitive light, let it out and shine it bright.

www.ingramcontent.com/pod-product-compliance
Lightning Source LLC
Chambersburg PA
CBHW051750130826
49812CB00033B/1084
* 9 7 8 9 3 5 7 4 4 2 5 4 1 *